Managing Projects with Make

Nutshell Handbooks

Nutshell Handbooks are concise, down-to-earth books on a variety of UNIX topics. Other books of interest are:

Using C on the UNIX System   218 pages, $24.95

There are C programmers and there are UNIX programmers. The difference is the knowledge of the system calls and special library routines available on UNIX. This book is for intermediate to experienced C programmers who want to become UNIX system programmers.

lex & yacc   210 pages, $24.95

This handbook describes how to use *lex* and *yacc* to develop simple-to-use tools that can improve overall productivity for programmers working on UNIX.

Checking C Programs with lint   82 pages, $12.95

If your programs are to have a chance of being portable to UNIXes or to other C-capable computers besides the particular one you use, there are only two choices: use lint or keep your code to yourself. *lint* verifies C program segments against standard libraries; checks for common portability errors; tests code against guidelines. This handbook explains how to use *lint* effectively to improve C programs on UNIX.

Programming with curses   75 pages, $12.95

This handbook will help you make use of the *curses* library in your C programs. We have presented ample material on *curses* and its implementation in UNIX so that you understand the whole as well as its parts.

For orders or a free catalog of all our books, please contact us.

O'Reilly & Associates, Inc.

Creators and Publishers of Nutshell Handbooks
632 Petaluma Avenue, Sebastopol, CA 95472
1-800-338-6887 • overseas/local 1-707-829-0515
email: uunet!ora!nuts

Managing Projects
with Make

Steve Talbott

O'Reilly & Associates, Inc.
632 Petaluma Avenue
Sebastopol, CA 95472

Managing Projects with Make
by Steve Talbott

Nutshell Series Editor Tim O'Reilly

Copyright © 1990 O'Reilly & Associates, Inc.
All rights reserved.

Printed in the United States of America

Revision History

1986:	First Edition
Aug. 1987:	Minor corrections. Index added. Revised page design by Linda Lamb and Dale Dougherty.
July 1988:	Minor corrections.
October 1989:	Minor corrections.
March 1990:	Minor corrections.

Please address comments and questions in care of the publisher:

O'Reilly & Associates, Inc.
632 Petaluma Avenue
Sebastopol, CA 95472
in USA 1-800-338-6887
international +1 707-829-0515

UUCP: uunet!ora!nuts
Internet: nuts@ora.uu.com

[*]

Table Of Contents

Preface
Scope of This Handbook

make is a command generator. It generates a sequence of commands for execution by the UNIX shell. These commands most commonly relate to the maintenance of a set of files comprising a particular software development project. "Maintenance" refers to a whole array of tasks, ranging from status reporting and the purging of "junk" files, to building the final, executable version of a complex group of programs.

make is most naturally used to sort out dependency relations among files. Even relatively small software projects typically involve a number of files that depend upon each other in various ways. For example, a program must be linked from object files and libraries, which in turn must be created from assembly language or high-level language source files. If you modify one or more source files, you must re-link the program after re-compiling some—but not necessarily all—of the sources. This process is normally repeated many times during the course of a project.

It is this process that *make* greatly simplifies. By recording once and for all the specific relationships among a set of files, you can thereafter let *make* automatically perform all updating tasks. You need only issue a command having this general form:

```
$ make myprog
```

make then carries out only those tasks necessitated by project work since the previous *make* command. It achieves this in part by examining the file system to determine when the relevant files were last modified. If file A depends on file B, and if file B was modified after file A, then file A must be "re-made"—compiled, linked, edited, substituted in a library, or whatever.

The Value of *make*

The UNIX operating system earned its reputation above all by providing an unexcelled environment for software development. The *make* and *sccs* utilities are widely regarded as the greatest contributors to the efficiency of this environment. The amount of time it takes you to learn the basics of *make* may not greatly exceed the amount of time you save every time you find yourself typing the command,

```
$ make myprog
```

There is one other point to make here. The modern software development environment is centered on teamwork. Many projects are too big for any one individual to handle. By keeping track of dependency relationships among the parts of large, complex projects, *make* helps coordinate the efforts of many contributors. It is an essential element in many software development undertakings.

Scope of This Handbook

This handbook is designed to teach you all the main features of the augmented version of *make* distributed with AT&T System V UNIX. This is the same version present in Berkeley UNIX distributions. Once you have studied this handbook, you will find that you can take advantage of all the main features of *make*, as well as many of the more obscure ones.

Chapter 1 explains the basic elements of a *make* description file, and leads you step by step through the creation of a simple description file. It explains the terms *target* and *component*, and discusses the commands *make* generates. After reading this chapter, you will be able to use *make* for many of its typical purposes.

Chapter 2 discusses macros and shell variables, and explains how the shell environment affects description files. This chapter includes information about some of *make*'s internal macros.

Chapter 3 covers the rather large subject of suffix lists and suffix rules. Understanding this material will enable you to see how *make* accomplishes so much of its work automatically, as if by "magic." You will learn how to write your own suffix rules.

Chapter 4 provides an overview of *make* command usage, command-line options, and special description file targets. It also gives some trouble-shooting hints for dealing with unexpected messages from *make*.

Chapter 5 details various out-of-the-way subjects and advanced topics. These include the method for invoking *make* recursively, the features designed for maintaining libraries, and additional capabilities of macros.

The booklet concludes with a quick-reference guide to all *make* features, and an example of a large description file.

1

How to Write
a Simple Makefile
The Description File
Invoking *make*
More about Dependency Lines
Commands

The command,

```
$ make program
```

indicates that you want to "make" a version—usually the latest
version—of *program*. That is, *program* is the **target** of the operation.
program typically depends on one or more files, called **components**.
Each of these files may in turn be targets with respect to yet other files
on which they depend. Therefore, before they can be used to "make"
program, they must themselves be made from their components. It is
this hierarchy of dependency relations that you must specify for *make*.
Once you have done so, a simple command like the one shown above
will guarantee that all necessary parts of the hierarchy are updated.
make, then, draws much of the information it needs from your
specification, or **description file**. This file is normally given the name,
makefile or *Makefile*. By default, *make* looks for a description file with
one or the other of these names (trying *makefile* first). In addition to
the description file, *make* derives necessary information from

filenames, from the "last-modified" times of files as recorded in the file system, and from a set of suffix rules.

The Description File

Suppose you are writing a program consisting of the following:

- three C language source files: *main.c, iodat.c, dorun.c.*
- assembly language code in *lo.s,* called by one of the C sources.
- a set of library routines in */usr/fred/lib/crtn.a.*

Here is a description file telling *make* all it needs to know:

```
1    program :  main.o iodat.o dorun.o lo.o \
              /usr/fred/lib/crtn.a
2         ld -o program main.o iodat.o dorun.o lo.o \
              /usr/fred/lib/crtn.a

3    main.o :  main.c
4         cc -c main.c
5    iodat.o :  iodat.c
6         cc -c iodat.c
7    dorun.o :  dorun.c
8         cc -c dorun.c
9  lo.o :  lo.s
10        as -o lo.o lo.s
```

(The numbers in the left margin are not part of the actual description file, but are added for convenience in explanation. Lines 1 and 2 are broken into two physical lines, as indicated by a backslash (\), to print them within the margins of this book. In the following explanation, lines 1 and 2 are referred to as single lines.)

This description file contains five entries. Each entry consists of a line containing a colon (the **dependency line**), and one or more **command lines** beginning with a tab. To the left of the colon on the dependency line are one or more targets; to the right of the colon are the component files on which the targets depend. The tab-indented command lines then show how to make the targets out of their components.

In the description file shown here, line 1 says that *program* depends on the files *main.o, iodat.o, dorun.o,* and *lo.o,* as well as on the library, */usr/fred/lib/crtn.a*. Line 2 specifies the linker command that makes *program* from its components. *make* will execute this command if *program* does not exist, or if any of the component files were modified after the "last-modified" date of *program*.

However, before executing the *ld* command, *make* first checks to see whether each of the components is up-to-date. The succeeding entries in the description file provide the information necessary to determine this. For example, line 3 shows that *main.o* depends on *main.c*; the compile command in line 4 will be executed (and a new *main.o* created) only if *main.c* was modified after the last time *main.o* was made. Similarly, *make* ensures that the other .o files are current with respect to their sources. Only after all these subordinate dependencies have been checked out and all the components of *program* brought up to date, will *make* execute the command shown in line 2.

make ignores blank lines in description files. Likewise, characters from a pound sign (#) to the end of a line are ignored, so that the pound sign designates the beginning of a comment. (However, do not place a pound sign immediately after an initial tab. If there is a tab, there must also be a command.) Lines containing an equals sign (=) are macros. (See Chapter 2 for a full discussion of macros.) Commands need not occupy separate lines in the description file; you can place a command on a dependency line, preceded by a semicolon:

```
target1 : comp1 comp2; command1
```

Chapter 2 and subsequent chapters will show how the description file used in this example can be greatly simplified.

Invoking *make*

The example in the previous section assumes that:

• The project files, as well as the description file, reside in the same directory.

- The description file is named *makefile* or *Makefile*.
- The directory containing these files will be the current directory when the command,

  ```
  $ make program
  ```

  is given.

make issues the message,

```
'program' is up to date
```

if no component files were modified since the last time *program* was created. Otherwise, each command line associated with *program* in the description file is echoed to the standard output (your terminal) and then executed. If, on the other hand, you attempt to make a target that is not contained in the description file and not covered by the default rules discussed in Chapter 3, *make* will respond like this:

```
$ make nontarget
make:  Don't know how to make nontarget.  Stop.
```

or like this:

```
$ make nontarget
'nontarget' is up to date.
```

The section on "Trouble-shooting" in Chapter 4 will help you understand the reason for the different messages.

Finally, you can say simply,

```
$ make
```

with no target name. In this case, the first target contained in the description file is made (together, of course, with all its components).

You need not make the highest-level target in a hierarchy of dependencies. Reverting to our makefile as described earlier, we could say,

```
$ make lo.o
```

to ensure that the file, *lo.o*, was up-to-date with respect to *lo.s*.

It is also possible to give *make* several targets in a single invocation:

```
$ make main.o dorun.o lo.o
```

make has many command-line options. For example, you can suppress echoing of command lines, cause errors returned by invoked commands to be ignored, or prevent actual execution of commands. These and other options are discussed in detail in Chapter 4.

More about Dependency Lines

A dependency line in a description file lists both targets and components, separated by a colon. These names may contain at least as many characters as the longest file names on your system, and must consist only of letters, digits, periods, and slashes (after any macros are interpreted—see Chapter 2). More than one target may depend on the same components:

```
target1 target2 : comp1 comp2 comp3
        command1
        command2
```

Suppose, however, that `target1` depends on all three components, but that `target2` depends only on `comp1` and `comp2`. While the dependency line shown here will work, it is not efficient, since invoking *make* will cause `target2` to be re-made if `comp3` has changed, even though `target2` does not actually depend on `comp3`. One natural-appearing remedy would be to structure the description file this way:

```
target1 target2 : comp1 comp2
        commands
target1 : comp3
        commands
```

(Here the two sets of commands are assumed to be different.) But *make* allows a target to be associated with only a single set of commands, if you use the syntax shown here. Therefore, this example is incorrect. One solution is to use the "double-colon" syntax:

```
target1 target2 :: comp1 comp2
        commands
target1 :: comp3
        commands
```

The double colon allows you to list the same target on two or more dependency lines, and to associate commands with each line. The double colon must appear on each of the dependency lines containing a target that is specified more than once. In other words, a target may appear on more than one dependency line, but all of those lines must be of the same (single- or double-colon) type. And if a target appears on more than one single-colon line, only one of those lines may have commands associated with it. This occurrence of targets on multiple, single-colon lines is merely a notational convenience for clarifying complex description files. *make* concatenates into a single dependency list all the components following each occurrence of the repeated target, so that it is as if you had specified a single dependency line with a single set of associated commands. That is, the entry,

```
target1 : comp1 comp2
        commands
target1 : comp3 comp4
```

is identical to the entry,

```
target1 : comp1 comp2 comp3 comp4
        commands
```

Note, finally, that in the current example there is another straight-forward solution—one that uses only single-colon dependency lines. This solution hinges on the fact that the same components can exist on any number of dependency lines:

```
target1 : comp1 comp2 comp3
        commands
target2 : comp1 comp2
        commands
```

Commands

When *make* executes a command associated with a target, it either does so directly, or else invokes the Bourne shell upon the command. The latter is the case whenever certain special characters requiring shell processing occur in the command—as, for example, input/output redirection symbols. The general intent is to obtain maximum speed (avoiding shell invocation whenever possible) but at the same time to make everything look like normal shell processing from the user's point of view. In the following description file entry, the first two commands will be consigned to the shell, while *make* itself will execute the third:

```
report : datafile1 datafile2 awkfile
     sort -bdf datafile1 datafile2 > /usr/tmp/rptxxx
     awk -f awkfile /usr/tmp/rptxxx > report
     rm /usr/tmp/rptxxx
```

Pipes are allowed, so this same entry could be written more simply:

```
report : datafile1 datafile2 awkfile
     sort -bdf datafile1 datafile2 | awk -f \
awkfile > report
```

In general, you can use any legitimate shell commands in your description file. However, each command must be only a single line, which constrains your use of the shell language's multi-line constructs such as for i in . . . done. One way to circumvent this limitation is to use the backslash to prevent the shell's interpretation of newlines. For example, consider this admittedly useless description file entry:

```
test :
     echo "Begin"
     for i in 1 2 3; do \
          echo "testing..."; \
          echo "...done testing"; \
     done
     echo "End"
```

The middle four lines in the command portion of this entry comprise a single shell command. The backslashes suppress the normal interpretation of the newline, resulting in the four lines being considered as a single line. It is exactly as if you had typed the four lines (without the backslashes) as a single very long line—which is, incidentally, another way to stretch the one-line-per-command limitation.

Note that since the newlines are effectively removed from this for loop, none of the semicolons shown here is optional. Also, you see that a target need not be dependent upon even a single component. (The colon, however, *must* be present.) The command,

```
$ make test
```

will inevitably result in execution of the command script shown in the entry, as long as there is not an actual file named *test* in the current directory.

There is another restriction upon commands in description files. Since each command line is executed in a separate shell, the "built-in" shell commands do not have effects across newlines. Built-in commands are those that the shell carries out itself, without invoking another program. Consequently, a *cd* command, for example, will remain in effect *within* a single line, but not on the following line. That is, if you have this description file entry:

```
target1 : comp1 comp2
        cd newdir
        ls
        ...
```

it will not work as you might expect. The *ls* command will list the directory you were in when you invoked *make*, not *newdir*. This is because the shell that executes `cd newdir` disappears once the command is finished, and a new shell—not affected by the *cd*—executes the next command. To achieve the desired effect, you must instead do this:

```
target : comp1 comp2
        cd newdir; ls
        ...
```

Here, since a shell is invoked upon the entire command line, the *cd* remains in effect when the *ls* is executed.

Similarly, any shell variables set in one command line are not carried across to the next. Likewise, the built-in command, *exit*, does not abort an entire sequence of commands. In this entry,

```
test :
        echo "Begin"
        for i in 1 2 3; do \
            echo "testing..."; \
            echo "...done testing"; \
            exit; \
        done
        echo "End"
```

the *exit* command has no effect, since it only exits from the *current* command line (which is finished anyway), not from the entire set of commands.

In other words, you must not consider the command set associated with a given target to be a shell procedure. (You can, however, write a separate shell procedure which is then invoked from a description file.) In addition to the differences already mentioned, there is also the absence of the standard shell procedure variables such as $*, $#, and $!. Further, shell variables that are not part of the environment (including the loop variable in `for i in . . . done` loops) can only be referenced with the use of two dollar signs rather than one:

```
test :
     read word; echo $$word
     ...
```

Note that this would not work if instead we wrote:

```
test :
     read word
     echo $$word    # $$word evaluates to a null string
     ...
```

And again, we can write:

```
for i in *.c; do \
     echo $$i; \
     ...
```

This example causes all filenames with the **.c** suffix in the current directory to be echoed.

You must refer to the shell's environmental variables exactly as you refer to *make* macros, as described in Chapter 2.

Pattern-matching Characters

The shell's filename pattern-matching characters, *****, **?**, and **[ ]**, are expanded in command lines, as well as on the *right* side of the colon in dependency lines. Therefore, the description file entry:

```
program : *.o
     lpr *.c
     ...
file1.o : file1.c
     ...
file2.o : file2.c
     ...
...
```

will cause *make* to assume that *program* is dependent upon all files in the current directory with the **.o** suffix, and will print all the **.c** files whenever *program* needs to be re-made.

2

Macros

Shell Variables
Internal Macros

Description file entries of the form

```
name = string
```

are macro definitions. Subsequent references to

```
$(name)
```

are interpreted as

```
string
```

More strictly, a macro definition is a line containing an equals sign and not preceded by a colon or tab. Macro definitions can be up to several hundred characters long. You cannot define macros dynamically in command scripts; their definitions become fixed before command execution begins. Typically, macro definitions are grouped together at the beginning of the description file. The name (string of letters and digits) to the left of the equals sign is assigned the string of characters following the equals sign. Blanks and tabs immediately to the left and right of the equals sign are ignored. As a general rule you should avoid characters special to the shell in your macro string definitions.

These are valid macro definitions:

```
COMPILER=/usr/fred/bin/cc
files     =       comp1 comp2 comp3
23 = "This is the (23)rd run"
FLAGS = -o -A -l 77
LIBES = /usr/fred/lib/maclib
OPT =
```

A macro that is never explicitly defined, or has no `string` to the right of the equals sign (like `OPT` above), is assigned the null string. It is permissible to include macros in macro definitions, as in

```
ABC = XYZ
FILE = TEXT.$(ABC)
```

References to `$(FILE)` will then evaluate to `TEXT.XYZ`. This is true regardless of the order in which the macros are defined.

Given the macro definitions shown above, a description file entry might look like this:

```
target : $(files)
        cmdfile $(FLAGS) $(LIBES) $(files)
```

You can use braces, "{ }", instead of parentheses in macro references. Single-character macro names do not require either parentheses or braces, although it is a good habit to use parentheses anyway. In the case of the macro definition,

```
A = XYZ
```

the references, $A, $(A) and ${A}, are identical.

A macro referred to in a dependency line must have been defined previous to the reference; otherwise, the reference will yield a null string. On the other hand, macros referred to in command lines may be defined at a point in the description file *following* the reference. In the latter case the macro substitution will still be successful.

Shell Variables

Shell variables that were part of the environment when you invoked *make* are available as macros within description files. However, you must refer to them using parentheses or braces (as described in the preceding section) whenever their names consist of more than one character. Therefore, if you have typed this variable definition to the shell before invoking make:

```
$ DIR=/usr/fred; export DIR
```

then you can access DIR from your description file:

```
target : comp1 comp2
     cd $(DIR); ...
```

C shell users can add shell variables to the environment with the setenv command:

```
% setenv DIR /usr/fred
```

Thus, any environmental variables you have set in your *.profile* or *.login* file—or by any other means—are available within description files.

Note the difference between these environmental variables, which are available as macros, and the limited possibility for use of dynamically assigned shell variables discussed at the end of Chapter 1. The latter require a double dollar sign, must not have parentheses or braces, and are ineffectual across newlines.

You can define macros on the *make* command line. The invocation,

```
make target1 DIR=/usr/fred
```

assigns the string /usr/fred to the name DIR; the string can then be accessed within the description file as $(DIR).

Priority of Macro Assignments

There are, we have seen, several sources for macro definitions accessible within description files: the current shell environment, command-line definitions, and the description file itself. In addition, *make* has its own definitions which are in effect by default. These may vary from one installation to the next. You can learn what they are for your system by typing this command to the Bourne shell:

```
$ make -fp - < /dev/null 2> /dev/null
```

This prints out all current and default macro definitions that *make* knows about, as well as a good deal of other information that we will explain later. The macro definitions occur at the head of the listing and include your current environmental variables. Here is a typical set of definitions, showing only the default values assigned by *make*:

```
GFLAGS =
GET = get
ASFLAGS =
AS = as
FFLAGS =
FC = f77
CFLAGS = -O
CC = cc
LDFLAGS =
LD = ld
LFLAGS =
LEX = lex
YFLAGS =
YACC = yacc
MAKE = make
MAKEFLAGS = b
```

We will see in the next chapter how these definitions are used in a set of default description file entries called "suffix rules."

With several sources for macro definitions, the question of priority becomes crucial: in the case of conflicting definitions, which ones govern while

make is executing? That is, if DIR is defined to be /usr/fred in the description file, but is defined as /usr/fred/lib in the current shell environment, which definition will *make* actually use? Here, then, is the order of priority, from least to greatest:

1. Internal (default) definitions of *make*.
2. Current shell environmental variables.
3. Description file macro definitions.
4. Command-line variable definitions.

By looking at the description file, you can determine without ambiguity what will happen when you invoke *make*. What you see in the file will not be overridden by the relatively "hidden" shell environment or the default definitions, but only by what you yourself type on the *make* command line.

However, there may be circumstances in which you would like the environment to overrule the description file. In such cases you can give the −e flag to *make*, with the result that the following becomes the order of priority:

1. Internal (default) definitions of *make*.
2. Description file macro definitions.
3. Current shell environmental variables.
4. Command-line variable definitions.

When you use the -e flag, the shell's environmental variables override any conflicting definitions in the description file. Therefore, given the description file entry,

```
TESTER = stdtest
test : srcfile
      $(TESTER) srcfile
```

the command line

```
$ make test
```

executes the command

```
stdtest srcfile
```

On the other hand, the command line

```
TESTER=newtest make -e test
```

executes the command

```
newtest srcfile
```

Internal Macros

make defines several "internal macros" that can simplify your description files. Three of these macros are defined as follows.

$?

$? evaluates to the **list of components that are younger** (more recently modified) **than the current target.** Suppose you have the description file entry,

```
target : comp1 comp2 comp3
    chmod +w $?
    [commands]
```

If you are making `target` and if `target` is out-of-date with respect to both `comp1` and `comp3`, then the first command line shown in this entry evaluates to

```
chmod +w comp1 comp3
```

$@

$@ evaluates to the **current target name**—that is, the target being "made." Therefore, if you have the description file entry,

```
target1 target2 : comp1 comp2 comp3
    cmdf $? > $@
```

and if `target1` is out-of-date with respect to `comp1` and `comp2`, while `target2` is out-of-date with respect to `comp3`, then the command line becomes

```
cmdf comp1 comp2 > target1
```

when `target1` is being made, while it becomes

```
cmdf comp3 > target2
```

when `target2` is being made.

$$@

$$@ has meaning *only* on dependency lines. (`$?` and `$@` can be used only in description file command lines.) `$$@` refers to exactly the same thing as `$@`—namely, **the current target** Thus, the description file entry,

```
docmk : $$@.c
```

becomes

```
docmk : docmk.c
```

This is useful for building large numbers of executable files, each of which has only one source file. For instance, the UNIX command directory could have a description file like this:

```
CMDS = cat dd echo date cc cmp comm ar ld chown
$(CMDS) : $$@.c
    $(CC) -O $? -o $@
```

Typing the command,

```
$ make echo
```

then becomes the same as if you had the description file entry:

```
echo : echo.c
    cc -O echo.c -o echo
```

Similarly, if you type

```
$ make cat date cmp ar
```

make builds each target in turn, with `$$@` evaluating to *cat* while *cat* is the target, to *date* while *date* is the target, and so on.

There are additional internal macros not described here. You will encounter them in Chapters 3 and 5.

In light of all this, our original description file from Chapter 1 becomes rather simpler:

```
OBJS = main.o iodat.o dorun.o lo.o
LIB = /usr/fred/lib/crtn.a

program : $(OBJS) $(LIB)
    ld -o $@ $(OBJS) $(LIB)

main.o : main.c
    cc -c $?

iodat.o : iodat.c
    cc -c $?

dorun.o : dorun.c
    cc -c $?

lo.o : lo.s
    as -o $@ $?
```

You might have thought that the *ld* command in this file could have had $? in the place of $(OBJS). However, $? represents only those component files that are more recently modified than the target, whereas the *ld* command must operate on *all* the object modules comprising the program.

3

Suffix Rules

How Suffix Rules Work
Types of Suffix Rules
Writing Your Own Suffix Rules

Even the simplified description file at the end of Chapter 2 can be reduced further. This is made possible by the existence of naming and compiling conventions. In UNIX programming environments, C language source files always have a **.c** suffix—a requirement imposed by the *cc* compiler. Similarly, FORTRAN source files have a **.f** suffix, and assembly language source files have a **.s** suffix. Furthermore, the C and FORTRAN compilers automatically place object modules into **.o** files.

Such conventions make it possible for *make* to do many tasks by acting upon a set of **suffix rules**. Relying upon these rules, we can simplify our sample description file to the following:

```
OBJS = main.o iodat.o dorun.o lo.o
LIB = /usr/fred/lib/crtn.a

program  :   $(OBJS) $(LIB)
     ld -o $@ $(OBJS) $(LIB)
```

While building *program*, *make* first checks to see whether *main.o* is up-to-date. It does this by looking for any file in the current directory that, according to standard suffix rules, could be used to make *main.o*. If it finds a file, *main.c*, and if that file has been changed since *main.o* was last made, *make* applies one of its rules by invoking the C compiler on *main.c*. Or if *make* finds a file, *main.f*, that is more recent than *main.o*, it invokes the FORTRAN compiler. Similarly with the assembler and *.s* files. It so happens that in the case of our sample description file, the default rules are sufficient to perform all the updating tasks except the *ld* command given explicitly in the description file. This description file allows you to type not only

```
$ make program
```

but also permits

```
$ make iodat.o
```

and so on, since the subordinate targets are covered by default rules.

By knowing the default suffix rules, or by defining your own suffix rules, you can greatly reduce the complexity of your description files.

How Suffix Rules Work

In effect, suffix rules amount to predefined, somewhat generalized description file entries. Here is how the rules our example draws upon are in fact defined:

```
.SUFFIXES  :  .o .c .s
.c.o :
        $(CC) $(CFLAGS) $<
.s.o :
        $(AS) $(ASFLAGS) -o $@ $<
```

The macros used in the commands all receive default definitions, as described in Chapter 2, although you can override them. The `.SUF-FIXES` line has the form of a dependency line, but with a difference. The space- or tab-separated components on this line represent the suffixes that *make* will consider "significant." Upon encountering a filename with one of these suffixes while traversing the hierarchy of dependencies related to the current target—and in the absence of any explicit, user-supplied instructions regarding the file—*make* looks for an applicable suffix rule. Consider, for example, our simplified description file. When building *program, make* takes the following steps:

- Look at each of the component files given by $(OBJ) and $(LIB), and treat each of those files as a target in turn. That is, see whether any of the component files needs to be made before *program* is made. Remember, while *make* works from the top (original target) down in determining the hierarchy of dependencies, it always works from the bottom upward in actually modifying, or making, targets.

- *program* depends on *iodat.o*, among other files. When, in the process of evaluating the components of *program, make* looks at *iodat.o*, it first looks for a user-specified dependency line containing *iodat.o* as a target. Finding none, it notes that the **.o** suffix is "significant," and therefore looks for another file in the current directory that can be used to make *iodat.o*. Such a file must

  – have the same name (apart from suffix) as *iodat.o*.

  – have a significant suffix.

  – be able to be used in order to make *iodat.o* according to an existing suffix rule.

  In this case the file, *iodat.c* meets all the requirements. The suffix rule we need was given above, and is one of the default rules of *make:*

  ```
  .c.o :
      $(CC) $(CFLAGS) $<
  ```

  This rule describes how to make a **.o** file from a **.c** file. (Note that while the syntax is similar, it is not the same as for regular description file entries.) Here $< has a meaning akin to $?, except that $< can be used only in suffix rules. It evaluates to whatever "component" triggered the rule—that is, to *iodat.c*. The **.o** file can be considered the target of this rule, and the **.c** file the component.

- *make* goes ahead and executes the suffix rule for creating a new *iodat.o* only if:

  – there are no further dependencies that must be checked out first (is *iodat.c* dependent on any other files, either explicitly or according to suffix rules? The answer is "No").

    – *iodat.o* is actually outdated with respect to *iodat.c*.

- Finally, after going through this process for each file in $ (OBJ) and $ (LIB), *make* executes the *ld* command to re-create *program* only if *program* was out-of-date with respect to any files in its hierarchy of dependencies.

Internal Macros in Suffix Rules

We have just seen that $<, used in suffix rule commands, yields the name of the "component" that is being used to make the "target"—for example, the **.c** file in a **.c.o** rule. Another macro available only in suffix rule commands is $*, representing the filename part (without suffix) of the "component." The suffix rule command,

```
cp $< $*.tmp
```

therefore evaluates to

```
cp main.c main.tmp
```

if *main.c* is the "component" the rule is acting upon.

The $? macro, described in Chapter 2, cannot occur in suffix rules; it has meaning only in normal description file entries. The $@ macro, also described in Chapter 2, can be used in both types of entry.

Types of Suffix Rules

The suffix rules shown above describe how to make a file with one suffix out of a file with a different suffix. There are two other forms that suffix rules can take. One supports SCCS files, and the other supports targets with a single source file.

SCCS Files

(Skip this section if you are not using SCCS.)

SCCS stands for the UNIX "Source Code Control System." Files under SCCS control have the prefix, **s.**, followed by the filename. Thus, a C language source file under SCCS control might have the name, *s.dorun.c*. Suffix rules use tildes (˜) to identify SCCS files. For example, the default suffix rule,

```
.c˜.o :
        $(GET) $(GFLAGS) -p $< > $*.c
        $(CC) $(CFLAGS) -c $*.c
        rm -f $*.c
```

describes how to transform a C language source file under SCCS control into an object file. The tilde tells *make* that it must look for an SCCS file in order to satisfy the rule. You can consider the first half (**.c˜**) of the suffix pair to represent a file of the form, *s.filename.c*. However, the tilde convention is a rather makeshift one—designed to avoid changing the syntax of *make* for dealing with SCCS files. In reality, the tilde merely tells *make* to "get" *filename.c* from the SCCS-controlled *s.filename.c*, and then to proceed as if this were a **.c.o** rule—almost. If this were fully the case, then $< would represent *filename.c* and $* would represent *filename*. If, on the other hand, **.c˜** truly stood for an *s.filename.c* file, we would expect $< to become *s.filename.c* and $* to become *s.filename*. The truth is halfway between:

$<   evaluates to *s.filename.c*

$*   evaluates to *filename*

Given the default macro definitions, the first command of the suffix rule therefore expands to

```
get -p $< > $*.c
```

Therefore, if we have a file, *s.dorun.c* in the current directory, the command,

```
$ make dorun.o
```

will result in the execution of these commands:

```
get -p s.dorun.c > dorun.c
cc -O -c dorun.c
rm -f dorun.c
```

If there happened to be a file, *dorun.c* already present in the current directory, then what we know so far would dictate that the default **.c.o** suffix rule rather than the **.c˜.o** rule should be invoked. The reason for this is that **.c** occurs before **.c˜** in the default `.SUFFIXES:` list, and therefore *make* should try to satisfy the **.c.o** rule first. However, it so happens that there is another suffix rule:

```
.c~.c:
        $(GET) $(GFLAGS) -p $< > $*.c
```

Consequently, when *make* finds the file, *dorun.c*, it automatically checks whether this file needs to be regenerated from *s.dorun.c*. If *s.dorun.c* was the more recently modified of the two files, then *make* generates *dorun.c* anew from the SCCS source.

The Null Suffix

It is possible to define suffix rules using only a single suffix. For example, one of the default suffix rules reads this way:

```
.c:
        $(CC) -n -O $< -o $@
```

In essence, this tells how to make a file with a null suffix (for example, an executable program) from a file with a .c suffix. (You should imagine the null suffix to occur between the given suffix and the colon.) This rule obviates the need for dealing with object files in the case of commands built out of single source files. If the file, *program.c* exists in the current directory, and if the single-suffix rule shown above is in effect, then the command,

```
$ make program
```

runs the C compiler on *program.c* to create *program*, as follows:

```
cc -n -O program.c -o program
```

(The C compiler invocation, without a –c switch, results in an automatic invocation of *ld*.)

Since the suffix rule illustrated here is in fact one of the default rules, C programs depending on single source files can be "made" without using any description file at all. If, for example, you have a directory containing source files for the commands, *cat, dd, echo,* and *date* (all built out of single source files), you need only type,

```
$ make cat dd echo date
```

and all four source files will be run through the C compiler and *ld* according to the above rule.

Writing Your Own Suffix Rules

You can re-define both the list of significant suffixes and the rules that transform files of one suffix-type into files of a different suffix-type. The description file line,

```
.SUFFIXES : .q .w .t
```

adds the suffixes, **.q, .w,** and **.t** to the current list of suffixes, while the line,

```
.SUFFIXES :
```

deletes all currently recognized suffixes. Therefore, the two lines,

```
.SUFFIXES :
.SUFFIXES : .q .w .t
```

replace the current suffixes with **.q, .w,** and **.t**. Be sure there are spaces or tabs between each suffix on the .SUFFIXES line.

The order of suffixes in the list is meaningful. Suppose you have a suffix list that includes **.c, .f,** and **.o,** together with suffix rules that transform FORTRAN (**.f**) and C (**.c**) files to object files. Suppose further that the current directory includes the files, *main.c* and *main.f*. In the absence of an explicit description file rule prescribing how to make *main.o* out of one of the source files, which default rule will get invoked? The answer is that if **.c** occurs first in the list of suffixes, the **.c.o** will be invoked. If **.f** occurs first, the **.f.o** rule will be invoked. Such a conflict is not highly likely, but it is well to keep in mind that the order of suffixes does make a difference.

You can find out what the current default suffixes and suffix rules are at your installation by typing this command to the Bourne shell:

```
$ make -fp - < /dev/null 2> /dev/null
```

If instead you type,

```
$ make -p 2> /dev/null
```

you will see the suffix list as it stands in light of any changes you made to them in your description file. You will also see any suffix rules you have added, together with all the default rules. While these default rules remain defined, they have no effect except so far as they apply to suffixes that are "significant"—that is, suffixes that are in the current list of suffixes. Further, your own suffix rules override any default rules governing the same suffix pairs.

To define your own suffix rules, you simply add the rules to your description file, just as if they were normal description file entries. For example, if you want *make* to help you maintain a set of text files that require formatting and printing, you could add suffixes and define suffix rules in a description file such as the one that is shown on the next page.

```
.SUFFIXES :
.SUFFIXES : .s .t .l .a

TBL = tbl
EQN = eqn
NEQN = neqn
ROFFARGS =

.s.l :   # format nroff -ms source file for line printer
        $(TBL) $< | $(NEQN) | nroff -ms -e -Tlp -u5 \
$(ROFFARGS) > $*.l

.s.t :   # format nroff -ms source file for terminal
        $(TBL) $< | $(NEQN) | nroff -ms -e -Tlp \
$(ROFFARGS) | ul -i > $*.t

.s.a :   # format troff -ms source file for apple \
laser printer
        $(TBL) $< | $(EQN) | troff -ms -Tpsc \
$(ROFFARGS) > $*.a

##########################################################
# Here begins the specific description file for "book"
##########################################################
CHAPS = ch01 ch02 ch03 appa
FORMATTED = ch01.l ch02.l ch03.l app.l

book : $(FORMATTED)
        lpr $(FORMATTED)
        rm $(FORMATTED)

$(CHAPS) : $$@.l
        lpr $?
        rm $?
```

The first half of this description file defines a set of general-purpose rules that could be used in numerous description files governing documentation projects. The second half provides the specific additional information required for one specific project. The following paragraphs explain the entries in this file.

Assumptions Governing the Description File

This description file assumes that all document source files have a .s suffix, indicating their use of the –ms formatting macros. (You could define similar rules for transforming, say, .m files and .e files, on the assumption that .m files use -mm macros and .e files use –me macros. These formatting macros should not be confused with the *make* macros discussed in this booklet.) The description file further assumes that when source files are processed by *nroff* or *troff*, they will be placed in .l files if they were formatted for the line printer, in .t files if formatted for output to a terminal, or in .a files if formatted for a laser printer. All formatting jobs are run through the *tbl* and *eqn/neqn* preprocessors by default. Finally, *troff* is assumed to be device-independent *troff*.

New Suffixes

The first line of the description file nullifies the default suffix rules of *make*. The second line establishes four suffixes as significant. These suffixes are interpreted according to the conventions described in the preceding paragraph—because we will base our suffix rules on those same conventions. The reason we did not simply add these suffixes to the existing (default) suffix list is that there are conflicts between the two sets of suffixes. Also, it is not likely that any of the default suffix rules would be needed in a documentation project.

Suffix Rules

There are three entries defining suffix rules. Note that, while there must be spaces between each suffix in the .SUFFIXES list, there *must not* be a space between the two suffixes on the first line of a suffix rule. Moreover, the order of suffixes in these entries is crucial. For example, the first entry declares how to make a .l file out of a .s file—that is, it gives the rule for converting a source file containing –ms macros into a formatted output file appropriate for printing on a line printer. Likewise, the third entry shows how to create a .a file (for output to a laser printer) out of a .s file. In other words, if you want to think about these rules in the same way you think about regular description file entries, you must think of the second suffix as belonging to the "target" and the first suffix as belonging to the "component."

These rules allow *make* to carry out certain actions even in the absence of any more specific instructions. If your current directory contains a file called *ch01.s*, then these rules alone allow you to type,

```
$ make ch01.l
```

in which case the first suffix rule results in execution of this command:

```
tbl ch01.s | neqn | nroff -ms -e -Tlp -u5 > ch01.l
```

One reason for using the `$(TBL)`, `$(EQN)`, and `$(NEQN)` macros instead of specifying the preprocessors literally in the suffix rule command lines is that the macros allow users to set environmental variables that override the default definitions, as described in Chapter 2. This is why you will often see null macro definitions in description files, like `$(ROFFARGS)` in our example. This provides a convenient way for the user to insert his own arguments into the *nroff* or *troff* command that *make* generates, simply by setting an environmental variable before invoking *make -e*.

The Project-specific Portion

The rest of the description file is intended to govern a specific writing project—a book consisting of three chapters (*ch01.s ch02.s, and ch03.s*) and one appendix (*appa.s*). The book is printed only on a line printer. If no formatted (*.l*) files currently exist, then making the target book results in this execution sequence:

```
$ make book
        tbl -TX ch01.s | neqn | nroff -ms -e -Tlp \
-u5 > ch01.l
        tbl -TX ch02.s | neqn | nroff -ms -e -Tlp \
-u5 > ch02.l
        tbl -TX ch03.s | neqn | nroff -ms -e -Tlp \
-u5 > ch03.l
        tbl -TX app.s | neqn | nroff -ms -e -Tlp \
-u5 > appa.l
        lpr ch01.l ch02.l ch03.l appa.l
        rm ch01.l ch02.l ch03.l appa.l
$
```

Since book depends on several *.l* files, and since *make* knows how to create *.l* files from *.s* files according to the given suffix rules, this creation takes place automatically. No explicit description file entry is required for making *ch01.l*, *ch02.l*, and so on. Of course, if one or more of the .l files already exist and are up-to-date, they will not be re-made.

The final entry in our sample description file was given as

```
$(CHAPS) :  $$@.l
     lpr $?
     rm $?
```

This allows you to print one or more individual chapters of the book, like this:

```
$ make ch02 ch03
     tbl -TX ch02.s | neqn | nroff -ms -e -Tlp \
-u5 > ch02.l
     lpr ch02.l
     rm ch02.l
     tbl -TX ch03.s | neqn | nroff -ms -e -Tlp \
-u5 > ch03.l
     lpr ch03.l
     rm ch03.l
```

Here $$@ has evaluated to the current target (*ch02* and *ch03* successively). *These targets never exist as files.* That is, there is never a file called *ch01* or *ch02*. $?, as we indicated in Chapter 2, evaluates to the current list of components that are younger (more recently modified) than the current target. In this case it never references more than a single file, since the current target never has more than a single component. In particular, $? always evaluates to some .l file and will presumably always need updating, because a non-existent target is always considered to be out-of-date with respect to an existing file. (Observe that the .l file is removed as part of the command sequence.) If a .l file should happen to exist, the presence of a .s.l suffix rule tells *make* to compare the "last modified" dates of the .s and .l files to determine whether the .l file needs re-making.

Some Variations

Writing description files for documentation projects is challenging, since there are so many possible macro, intermediate file, and output device combinations. We could, for example, have written our first suffix rule this way instead:

```
.s.l :    # format nroff -ms source file & send to printer
       $(TBL) $< | $(EQN) | nroff -ms -e -Tlp -u5 | lpr
```

In this case the formatted file is automatically sent to the line printer, and no intermediate file is created. This means that a suffix rule can serve a useful purpose even if one of the suffixes never exists in an actual filename. Here the ".l file" is made by formatting a .s file and printing it. The relevant *make* command is

```
$ make ch01.l
```

This is really just another instance of the truth we already encountered: a target need not actually exist as a file.

If we want to be able to choose between generating an intermediate file or sending formatted output directly to a printer, we could formulate two rules for each macro / device combination:

```
.s.l :    # format nroff -ms source file for line printer
       $(TBL) $< | $(EQN) | nroff -ms -e -Tlp -u5 > $*.l
.s.lx :    # format nroff -ms source file & send to printer
       $(TBL) $< | $(EQN) | nroff -ms -e -Tlp -u5 | lpr
```

This illustrates that a suffix can have more than one letter. (The new suffix—.lx—must be added to the .SUFFIXES list.) With these rules, we could create a .l file from a .s file with

```
$ make ch01.l
```

or format and print a .s file with

```
$ make ch01.lx
```

4

Command-line Usage
and Special Targets

There are many ways to control and modify the normal actions of
make. In addition to the various command-line options, there are several pseudo-targets you can place in your description files, with a con-
sequent effect on *make's* behavior. This chapter discusses the many
ways to use the *make* command.

The Command Line

The *make* command accepts four types of arguments—macro
definitions, option flags, description file names, and target file names:

```
$ make [options] [targets] [macro definitions]
```

A description file name follows immediately after the **–f** option flag, as
indicated below. *make* first analyzes all macro definition arguments

and makes the assignments. While these definitions are shown at the end of the command line, they may actually occur anywhere except between the **–f** flag and the following file name. (In the case of the C shell they must not occur before the word "make.") Shell environmental macros may or may not override corresponding definitions given in the description files, depending on whether the **–e** option is specified (see Chapter 2). Next *make* analyzes the option flags which begin with hyphens. And finally, it takes the remaining arguments, in left-to-right order, as names of targets. If there are no such arguments, the first name in the description file that does not begin with a period is "made."

The **–f** option allows you to specify a description file with a non-standard name. For example, the command,

```
$ make -f term.mk iomod
```

tells *make* to use *term.mk* as a description file while generating the target, *iomod*. (Incidentally, the **.mk** suffix convention is useful whenever it is convenient to have more than one makefile in the same directory.) You can effectively combine multiple description files by using more than one **–f file** argument pair on the command line. In the absence of the **–f** option, *make* looks for one of the following files, in the order given: *makefile, Makefile, s.makefile, s.Makefile*. (The latter two are assumed to be under SCCS control: see "SCCS Files" in Chapter 3.) Finally, if you give a hyphen as the name of your description file:

```
$ make -f - target ...
```

make will read the description file from the standard input. This can be helpful for time-saving experimentation while you are learning how *make* works. *make* will not actually perform the tasks specified in the standard input "description file" until you type a CTRL-D, signifying end-of-file. This is because *make* always reads the entire description file before executing any commands.

Status Information and Debugging

make normally echoes to the standard output (your terminal) each command line that it executes. If you use the **–n** option, then *make* echoes the commands, but does not actually execute them. Therefore, the invocation

```
$ make -n target1 target2 ...
```

enables you to find out in just a second or two the current state of one or more dependency hierarchies—that is, one or more sets of related files. This invocation tells you how much work *make* will have to do in order to re-generate the targets. By saving the output of *make -n* in a script, you create a command file. Sometimes such a file proves useful when *make* gets interrupted part way through its task and you want to "manually" finish the task. You must, of course, create the script *before* running *make* without the **-n**.

Conversely, the command

```
$ make -s target1 target2 ...
```

executes all required commands, but does not echo them. You can achieve exactly the same effect by placing this pseudo-target anywhere in your description file:

```
.SILENT :
```

To prevent any single command from being echoed, give an 'at' sign (@) as the first character on the command line:

```
target : comp.c
    cc -O comp.c
    @ echo "Done"
```

Note, however, that even commands beginning with @ are echoed when you use the **-n** option.

The **-q** ("question") option instructs *make* to return a zero or non-zero status code, depending on whether the target files are up-to-date or not. You can sometimes use this feature to good advantage when invoking *make* from a shell command script:

```
make -q comp1 comp2
if [ "$?" != "0" ]; then
    date >> $(LOGFILE)
    ...
fi
```

Here $? is a shell variable containing the exit status of the immediately previous command. It is not part of a description file, but rather part of a normal shell procedure. Therefore it is not a *make* macro. Or again,

```
make -snq target
if [ "$?" = "0" ]; then
        make -st  target
else
        make -s target
fi
...
```

You will observe that command-line options for *make* can be grouped after a single hyphen (**–snq**). Also, the simultaneous presence of the **–s** and **–n** options results in repression of both command echoing and command execution. The **–t** ("touch") option causes *make* to change the last-modified date of the target to be the current date. This is a potentially dangerous option, inasmuch as it destroys *make's* record of the previous relations between files. In the above example, the **–t** option is given only if the target is already shown to be current; otherwise, the target is "made."

As described in Chapters 2 and 3, the **–p** option causes *make* to print out the complete set of macro definitions, suffixes, suffix rules, and description file entries. Much more detailed (and not necessarily understandable!) information results from the **–d** ("debug") option. In the output from this option, the message, "envflg = 0", indicates that the corresponding variable is not part of the shell environment, while "envflg = 1" signifies the opposite. (The use of the **–e** command-line option—enabling the environmental variables to override description file macro definitions—was described in Chapter 2.)

Error Handling

make normally stops if any command it generates returns a non-zero (error) exit code. Before quitting, however, it removes the current target it is making. The assumption here is that the target is probably in a partly finished state. If it were left in place, it would show as "up-to-date" in subsequent invocations of *make*, due to its now-revised date of last modification.

There may be occasions when you do not want the target removed upon occurrence of errors. The .PRECIOUS: pseudo-target allows you to specify any files you do not want destroyed. For example, the description file entry

```
.PRECIOUS :   target1 target2 target3
```

prevents any of the three named targets from being removed by *make*. This entry can occur anywhere in the description file.

The –i option instructs *make* to ignore error codes returned by the commands it generates. In this case, *make* goes ahead and executes every command it can, regardless of the fact that one of those commands may have failed. Needless to say, this can be dangerous, raising the possibility that a faulty component of a software project will be created, while erasing information about the previous dependency relations between files. The effect of the –i option can also be achieved by placing the .IGNORE: pseudo-target anywhere in the description file. More selectively, you can tell *make* to ignore the return codes of particular commands by prefacing the commands with a hyphen (–):

```
target :   comp
       - echo "Beginning to make target" > /dev/tty2
       ...
```

Less dangerous than the –i option and .IGNORE: is the –k option. It causes *make* to abandon work on the current target when a command returns a non-zero exit status, but to continue work on all other targets not dependent on the current entry. Therefore, everything that can correctly be updated will be updated, while other targets will remain untouched. *make* tells you what it does not regenerate in this case. For example, consider the description file entries,

```
target :   comp1 comp2 comp3
       [commands]

comp1 :
       [commands]

comp2 :
       [commands]

comp3 :
       [commands]
```

If make -k target encounters an error while updating *comp1*, it immediately ceases its work on this branch of the hierarchy of dependencies. However, *make* continues to work on *comp2* and *comp3*. When this work is finished and it is time to regenerate *target* from its three component files, *make* recognizes that one of the components could not be made, and therefore does not attempt to execute the commands for creating *target*.

The MAKEFLAGS Macro

make automatically defines a macro, MAKEFLAGS, containing the command-line option flags given in the current invocation of *make*. For example, if you invoked *make* with the command,

```
$ make -kqsf target.mk target
```

then the description file entry

```
target :
        echo $(MAKEFLAGS)
```

would result in the output

```
kqs
```

(The **–f, –p,** and **–r** option flags do not show up in the MAKEFLAGS macro.) Judging from conventional UNIX documentation, the intent was that MAKEFLAGS could be redefined in a description file, and that the presence of a shell variable named MAKEFLAGS would be used by *make* to set command-line options at start-up time. The current value of MAKEFLAGS would then affect recursive invocations of *make*, as described in Chapter 5. However, there is some question whether existing implementations of *make* allow either environmental or description file definitions of the MAKEFLAGS macro to work. The effect of such definitions may in some cases even be to abort otherwise correct executions of *make*. Before deciding to use these features, you should experiment with the version of *make* on your system. If portability is a concern, it would be best not to use MAKEFLAGS.

Additional Features

The **–r** option has an effect similar to . SUFFIXES : without a suffix list: it causes *make* to ignore the default rules. One difference, however, is that **–r** results in a warning message from *make* (unless you also specify **–s** or . SILENT :)—

```
No suffix list.
```

The **–b** option is, in most implementations, on by default. It assures backward compatibility with earlier versions of *make*, so that old description files continue to work.

Commands associated with the .DEFAULT: pseudo-target will be executed if a file must be made but there are no relevant description file entries or suffix rules. For example:

```
.DEFAULT :
      ls -l
      echo "No commands to execute"
```

Trouble-shooting

The messages issued by *make* can prove bewildering until you become familiar with certain rules. For the most part, *make* is content to respond in one of three ways whenever it does not actually execute a series of commands:

√ **Make: Don't know how to make target. Stop.**

You will receive this message if you type

```
$ make target
```

at a time when all the following are true:

- *target* does not exist as a file in your current directory.
- *target* also does not exist as a target in your description file.
- No suffix rule applies to the combination of *target* and some file in the current directory.

You will receive a similar message if some specified component of the target fulfills the same three conditions. For example, suppose you have the entries,

```
target :  comp1 comp2
      [commands]

comp1 :  file1
      [commands]
```

but do not have an entry in which *comp2* appears as a target. Then you will get this response:

```
$ make target
[echoed commands for making comp1]
Make.  Don't know how to make comp2.  Stop.
```

There is, however, a *nearly* identical case where you get a quite different message—which brings us to the next message.

√ 'target' is up to date.

If *target* has no components specified in a description file entry (it may not even have a description file entry), *but does exist as a file in the current directory*—and if no current suffix rules apply to this file— then *make* tells you the target is up-to-date. This proves especially puzzling when the target does have a description file entry, but has no associated components. Normally, you want such a target—when it is being made—to result in a specific command sequence without variation. For example, you might have the entry,

```
print :
     pr *.c
```

Indeed, a `make print` command will inevitably cause the *pr* line to execute—*unless you happen to have a file called print* in the current directory. If such a file exists, *make* will simply tell you that it is up-to-date, regardless of any other considerations.

Consider again the description file entries discussed above:

```
target :  comp1 comp2
     [commands]

comp1 :   file1
     [commands]
```

This caused the message,

```
Make.  Don't know how to make comp2.  Stop.
```

when *comp2* did not exist as a file or target. However, if *comp2* does exist as a file, and if neither current suffix rules nor an explicit description file entry tell how to make it, *make* automatically assumes it is up-to-date. Therefore, the command,

```
$ make target
```

should result in a successful generation of *target*.

√ **The third response** *make* may give is absolute silence—it just returns a prompt sign. This may indicate a missing component file. If, for example, you have the description file entry,

```
main :  main.o
```

and then type

```
$ make main
```

make will check whether *main.o* is up-to-date with respect to *main.c*, according to the standard **.c.o** suffix rule. Everything proceeds normally if *main.c* (or *main.f* or any other file from which *make* knows how to generate *main.o*) exists in the current directory. But if:

- such a file does not exist;
- *main.o* does exist;
- *main* either does not exist or was modified before the last time *main.o* was modified;

then the *make* command shown will return with no message. The reason is that, since *main* is specified as a target in the description file, and since no suffix rules are found that apply to *main.o* and any other file in the current directory, *make* considers that it has successfully generated *main* by carrying out the commands given in the explicit description file entry. Since there are no such commands (in effect, there is a null command), nothing is echoed, *make* considers its job done, and returns the prompt. Of course, if *main* existed and was younger than *main.o*, you would have received instead the message,

```
'main' is up to date.
```

Explicit Rules vs. Default Rules

There is one other situation that can cause puzzling results. Suppose there is a file, *main.c*, in the current directory. Then consider this description file entry:

```
main.o :
```

Since *main.o* now occurs as a target in an explicit description file entry, does that effectively nullify the default rule that would allow *make* to generate *main.o* from *main.c*? In other words, will the command

```
$ make main.o
```

now result in the default *cc* command if *main.c* has been modified more recently than *main.o*? Or will no command be executed at all, since we have specified *main.o* explicitly in the description file, but given no commands for making it? The answer is that the default rule will still be applied—*but only so long as no commands are associated with the description file entry*. If instead we had

```
main.o :
        echo hello there
```

the command to "`make main.o`" would result in the echo, and the default *cc* command would effectively be nullified. (Of course, as discussed above, if *main.o* already exists in the current directory, any attempt to make it will result only in the message that it is up-to-date. The echo occurs only when it is actually necessary to re-generate *main.o*.)

Syntax Errors

make will report a syntax error upon encountering a violation of proper description file format. A missing colon on a target line, or a missing tab on a command line are examples of such violations. Both these errors will yield a message like this:

```
Make: Must be a separator on line 5. Stop
```

A more difficult problem to locate consists merely of a stray tab character in the description file. For example, a "hidden" line consisting only of a tab—if the line appears any place where a command is not expected—generates the message:

```
Make: line 3: syntax error. Stop.
```

Infinitely Recursive Macros

If your description file contains the macro definition,

```
FILE = XXX${FILE}
```

then executing *make* with this description file will yield the message,

```
Make: infinitely recursive macro?. Stop.
```

Alternatively, this condition may simply result in an abort of *make* and a core dump. While it is permissible to refer to one macro in the definition of another, a macro must not refer to itself.

5

Out-of-the-way Topics

More about Macros
Maintaining Libraries
Recursive Invocation of *make*

This chapter explains a number of the less common and more advanced features of *make*. These include some additional aspects of internal macros; library maintenance; and recursive invocations of *make*.

More about Macros

All internal macros except $? can take a D or F suffix. These have the effect of truncating file pathnames referred to by the macros; D truncates the pathname so that only the directory portion of the name remains, while F truncates to the file portion of the name. If, for example, $@ currently represents /usr/include/file.h, then $(@F) evaluates to file.h and $(@D) evaluates to

/usr/include. You might therefore have the description file entries:

```
iomodule : /usr/fred/header/io.h /usr/fred/work/io.c
    cd $(<D); $(MAKE) $(<F)
mathmodule : /usr/fred/header/math.h /usr/fred/work/math.c
    cd $(<D); $(MAKE) $(<F)
...
```

Here $(MAKE) causes recursive execution of *make*, as described later in this chapter. With *iomodule* as a target, *make* first changes directory to */usr/fred/header* and does a "make io.h". Next it changes directory to */usr/fred/work* and does a "make io.c".

Both the F and D modifiers act on file pathnames containing slashes (/). If you use these modifiers with internal macros that do not contain slashes, the F modifier will yield the current value of the macro without modification, while the D modifier will produce a period (.), signifying the current directory.

Macro String Substitution

You can perform certain string substitutions upon all macros used in description file shell commands. Suppose you have the macro definition,

```
LETTERS = abcxyz
```

In this case, the command

```
echo $(LETTERS:xyz=def)
```

will produce the output,

```
abcdef
```

make will not substitute for *every* occurrence of the designated string. The substitution occurs only at the end of the macro, or immediately before white space. That is, the description file entries,

```
LETTERS = xyz xyzabc xyz
...
    echo $(LETTERS:xyz=def)
```

will produce the output,

```
def xyzabc def
```

The reason for this is that *make* is normally concerned with suffixes, and indeed the substitution feature of macros is most likely to prove useful in the transformation of suffixes. However, it is not a feature you will encounter frequently.

Maintaining Libraries

If a target or component contains parentheses (without a dollar sign), that target or component is assumed to be a library of object modules; the name inside the parentheses represents a member of the library. Thus, the target, `mylib(iomod1.o)`, is in actuality the library module, *iomod1*, part of *mylib*. The use of the .o suffix and the parentheses in this notation are oddities testifying to the fact that library handling was "tacked on" to *make* rather as an afterthought.

There can only be a single name inside the parentheses. Handle multiple modules by repeating the entire construct:

```
lib :   mylib(iomod1.o) mylib(iomod2.o)
mylib(testmod.o) ...
```

or better:

```
SRCS = mylib(iomod1.o) mylib(iomod2.o)
mylib(testmod.o) ...
...
lib : $(SRCS)
...
```

(Note that the target, *lib*, does not represent an actual file here.) In effect, `mylib(iomod1.o)` represents the module as it stands in the library. Updating this module therefore means regenerating *mylib* with a current version of `iomod1` taken from *iomod1.o*. The default rule for updating library modules in this way is

```
.c.a :
        $(CC) -c $(CFLAGS) $<
        ar rv $@ $*.o
        rm -f $*.o
```

(You must check the default rules at your installation, as described in Chapter 3, to make sure this suffix rule has not been changed.) The idea behind this rule is that targets and components containing parentheses are arbitrarily considered by *make* to be an abstraction called ".a files"—not necessarily having anything to do with real **.a** files—and therefore can bring the rule into play. It is a peculiarity of the current implementation of *make* that `mylib(iomod1.o)` cannot be made to depend on *iomod1.o*; that is why the suffix rule transforms **.c** files (rather than **.o** files) into library modules. In light of the suffix rule, you can maintain a three-member library with this description file entry:

```
lib :   mylib(iomod1.o) mylib(iomod2.o) mylib(iomod3.o)
        @ echo "mylib is now up-to-date"
```

When attempting to generate *mylib* in this entry, *make* first considers each component in turn. The occurrence of the parentheses tells *make* to construe *mylib(iomod1.o)*, for example, as if it contained a **.a** suffix. Given such a suffix, together with the **.c.a** suffix rule and a file in the current directory called *iomod1.c*, *make* can regenerate *mylib(iomod1.o)* by executing the commands associated with the suffix rule. The net effect is to place a current version of *iomod1* into *mylib*. (This will be done, however, only if the **.c** file was changed later than its executable version in *mylib*.) After updating the other two library modules in similar fashion, *make* executes the *echo* command associated with the target, *mylib*.

The key to understanding the whole procedure is to realize that the construct, *mylib(iomod1.o)* is interpreted by *make* as if it had a **.a** suffix, triggering the **.c.a** suffix rule. This assumption has nothing to do with any actual **.a** suffix in the targets or components. The target could be given as *mylib.a* and the components as *mylib.a(iomod1.o)*, and so on, without the explicit suffixes having any effect on *make*. It is only the parentheses that alert *make* to the presence of ".a" files.

While building *mylib*, *make* at first sets its internal macros as follows:

```
$@  =   mylib
$<  =   iomod1.c
$*  =   iomod1
```

As each component is successively treated, `$<` and `$*` change accordingly. `$?` is also defined, evaluating to the set of components (.o files) that have been changed since they were last incorporated into *mylib*. `$@` is not derived from the actual target, as is normally the case, but rather from the string to the left of the first parenthesis in the current component. In addition, there is yet one more internal macro we have not previously discussed: `$%` evaluates to whatever expression occurs inside the parentheses. In our example:

```
$%   = iomod1.o
```

Note that the special construct referring to library members can also occur as a target in description file entries:

```
lib :    mylib(iomod1.o) mylib(iomod2.o) mylib(iomod3.o)
         @ echo "mylib is now up-to-date"
mylib(iomod1.o) :    /usr/include/stdio.h
   ...
```

In this case, *mylib* will be updated if */usr/include/stdio.h* has been changed since the last time time *iomod1* was incorporated into the library. The command line for making a particular module (that is, updating it in the library) requires that you escape the parentheses to protect them from the shell:

```
$ make lib\(iomod1.o\)
```

Finally, here is a slightly different approach to maintaining the same library:

```
lib :    mylib(iomod1.o) mylib(iomod2.o) mylib(iomod3.o)
         $(CC) -c $(CFLAGS) $(?:.o=.c)
         ar rv mylib $?
         rm $?
         @ echo "mylib is now up-to-date"
 .c.a:
         ;
```

The main difference here is that all necessary **.o** modules are regenerated with a single invocation of the C compiler, saving a good deal of time. Suffix rules cannot accomplish the same thing, since they must make one target at a time. In order for this new approach to work, however, the default suffix rule has to be nullified, preventing *make* from compiling each module, one at a time. The suffix rule still gets invoked for each component of the library that is out-of-date, but this results only in execution of a null command in each case. The use of the `$(?:.o=.c)` construction causes **.o** names to become **.c** names through macro string substitution, as described in Chapter 4.

If `$(CC)` equals `cc` and `$(CFLAGS)` equals `-O`, and if all three library modules need updating, then the first three commands of this description file entry become

```
cc -c -O iomod1.c iomod2.c iomod3.c
ar rv mylib iomod1.o iomod2.o iomod3.o
rm iomod1.o iomod2.o iomod3.o
```

Recursive Invocation of *make*

You can invoke *make* recursively. That is, a command in a description file entry can be another *make* command. A typical use for this is with very large software projects, where a master description file exists in a parent directory, and various relatively independent parts of the project have their own description files in sub-directories. The master description file might then look like this, in part:

```
INCRT = /usr/include
MACHINE =

system :
      cd os; make -f os.mk -k "CC=$(CC)" \
"INCRT=$(INCRT)" "MACHINE=$(MACHINE)"

network :
      cd net; make -f net.mk -k "CC=$(CC)" \
"INCRT=$(INCRT)" "MACHINE=$(MACHINE)"

drivers :
      cd io; make -f io.mk -k "CC=$(CC)" \
"INCRT=$(INCRT)" "MACHINE=$(MACHINE)"
```

In this example, the invocation of *make* from within the description file must provide its own command-line option flags, and must define *on the command line* any macros that were defined in the current description file and that should also be available in the description file for the newly invoked *make*. Of course, the *default* macro definitions will still obtain in the new instance of *make*. But if one of the default macros might have been re-defined by the user of the current instance of *make*, and if this re-definition should be carried across to the recursive instance, then the macro must be explicitly passed via the command line. That is why the CC=$(CC) argument occurs in the above example.

There is, however, another way to invoke *make* recursively. The $(MAKE) macro is automatically defined to mean "make"—but with a difference. If a description file entry reads

```
system :
     cd os; $(MAKE) -f os.mk -k "CC=$(CC)" \
"INCRT=$(INCRT)" "MACHINE=$(MACHINE)"
```

the result is exactly like what was just discussed, except that the recursive *make* command will execute even if the first *make* call included a –n option; and the command-line options (excluding –f, –p, and –r) of the first instance of *make* are automatically passed to the recursive instance. The result is that, with a single

```
$ make -n
```

command you can see all the required updating in an entire tree of related description files, not only in the topmost description file. This works because the –n option flag is automatically passed to the recursive *make*, together with any flags given in the recursive call. It is still the case, however, that you must explicitly pass new or possibly redefined macros to the new *make*.

Quick-Reference
Command Line

make [-f *descfile*] [*options*] [*targets*] [*macro definitions*]

Command-line Option Flags

–b   Accept description files from previous versions of *make*.

–d   Debug mode—print detailed information about internal flags
        and the last-modified times of files.

—e   Let environmental variables override macro definitions inside description files.

—f   Following argument is taken to be a description file.

—i   Ignore error codes. Same as `.IGNORE:` in description file.

—k   Error terminates work on current branch of hierarchy, but not on other branches.

—n   Echo command lines, but do not execute them. Even lines beginning with @ are echoed.

—p   Print out macro definitions, suffixes, suffix rules, and explicit description file entries.

—q   Return zero or non-zero status, depending on whether the target file is or is not up-to-date.

—r   Do not use the default rules.

—s   Do not echo command lines. Same as `.SILENT:` in description file.

—t   Touch target files (making them appear up-to-date), without executing any other commands.

Internal Macros

$?   The list of components that have been changed more recently than the current target. Can be used only in normal description file entries—not suffix rules.

$@   The name of the current target, except in description file entries for making libraries, where it becomes the library name. Can be used both in normal description file entries and suffix rules.

$<   The name of the current component which has been modified more recently than the current target. Can be used only in suffix rules and the `.DEFAULT:` entry.

$*   The name—without the suffix—of the current component that has been modified more recently than the current target. Can be used only in suffix rules.

$$@   The name of the current target. Can be used only to the right of the colon in dependency lines.

$%   The name of the corresponding .o file when the current target
           is a library module. Can be used both in normal description
           file entries and suffix rules.

Macro Modifiers

D   The directory portion of any internal macro except $?. For
           example, $(*D), $(<D), $(@D), $$(@D).

F   The file portion of any internal macro except $?. For
           example, $(*F), $(<F), $(@F) $$(@F).

Macro String Substitution

$(macro:abc=xyz)

           Evaluates to the current definition of $(macro), after sub-
           stituting the string xyz for every occurrence of abc that
           occurs either immediately before a blank or tab, or at the end
           of the macro definition.

Pseudo-targets

.DEFAULT: Commands associated with this pseudo-target will
               be executed if a legitimate target must be made but
               there are no applicable description file entries or
               suffix rules.

.IGNORE: Ignore error codes. Same as the –i option flag.

.PRECIOUS: Components you specify for this pseudo-target will
               not be removed when you send a signal (such as
               interrupt) that aborts *make*.

.SILENT: Execute commands but do not echo them. Same as
               the –s option flag.

Description File Command Codes

@   Do not echo this command line.

–   Ignore error return from this command.

B

Sample Default Macros, Suffixes, and Rules

```
EDITOR = /usr/bin/vi
TERM = tvi950ns
SHELL = /bin/csh
PATH = .:/bin:/usr/bin:/usr/fred:/usr/local
LOGNAME = fred
HOME = /usr/fred
GFLAGS =
GET = get
ASFLAGS =
AS = as
FFLAGS =
FC = f77
CFLAGS = -O
CC = cc
LDFLAGS =
LD = ld
LFLAGS =
LEX = lex
YFLAGS =
```

```
YACC = yacc
MAKE = make
$ = $
MAKEFLAGS = b

.h~.h:
        $(GET) $(GFLAGS) -p $< > $*.h
.s~.a:
        $(GET) $(GFLAGS) -p $< > $*.s
        $(AS) $(ASFLAGS) -o $*.o $*.s
        ar rv $@ $*.o
        -rm -f $*.[so]
.r~.a:
        $(GET) $(GFLAGS) -p $< > $*.r
        $(FC) -c $(FFLAGS) $*.r
        ar rv $@ $*.o
        rm -f $*.[ro]
.e~.a:
        $(GET) $(GFLAGS) -p $< > $*.e
        $(FC) -c $(FFLAGS) $*.e
        ar rv $@ $*.o
        rm -f $*.[eo]
.f~.a:
        $(GET) $(GFLAGS) -p $< > $*.f
        $(FC) -c $(FFLAGS) $*.f
        ar rv $@ $*.o
        rm -f $*.[fo]
.r.a:
        $(FC) -c $(FFLAGS) $<
        ar rv $@ $*.o
        rm -f $*.o
.e.a:
        $(FC) -c $(FFLAGS) $<
        ar rv $@ $*.o
        rm -f $*.o
.f.a:
        $(FC) -c $(FFLAGS) $<
        ar rv $@ $*.o
        rm -f $*.o
.c~.a:
        $(GET) $(GFLAGS) -p $< > $*.c
        $(CC) -c $(CFLAGS) $*.c
        ar rv $@ $*.o
        rm -f $*.[co]
```

```
.c.a:
     $(CC) -c $(CFLAGS) $<
     ar rv $@ $*.o
     rm -f $*.o

.l.c:
     $(LEX) $<
     mv lex.yy.c $@

.y~.c:
     $(GET) $(GFLAGS) -p $< > $*.y
     $(YACC) $(YFLAGS) $*.y
     mv y.tab.c $*.c
     -rm -f $*.y

.y.c:
     $(YACC) $(YFLAGS) $<
     mv y.tab.c $@

.l~.o:
     $(GET) $(GFLAGS) -p $< > $*.l
     $(LEX) $(LFLAGS) $*.l
     $(CC) $(CFLAGS) -c lex.yy.c
     rm -f lex.yy.c $*.l
     mv lex.yy.o $*.o

.l.o:
     $(LEX) $(LFLAGS) $<
     $(CC) $(CFLAGS) -c lex.yy.c
     rm lex.yy.c
     mv lex.yy.o $@

.y~.o:
     $(GET) $(GFLAGS) -p $< > $*.y
     $(YACC) $(YFLAGS) $*.y
     $(CC) $(CFLAGS) -c y.tab.c
     rm -f y.tab.c $*.y
     mv y.tab.o $*.o

.y.o:
     $(YACC) $(YFLAGS) $<
     $(CC) $(CFLAGS) -c y.tab.c
     rm y.tab.c
     mv y.tab.o $@

.s~.o:
     $(GET) $(GFLAGS) -p $< > $*.s
     $(AS) $(ASFLAGS) -o $*.o $*.s
     -rm -f $*.s

.s.o:
     $(AS) $(ASFLAGS) -o $@ $<
```

```
.r~.o:
        $(GET) $(GFLAGS) -p $< > $*.r
        $(FC) $(FFLAGS) -c $*.r
        -rm -f $*.r

.e~.e:
        $(GET) $(GFLAGS) -p $< > $*.e

.e~.o:
        $(GET) $(GFLAGS) -p $< > $*.e
        $(FC) $(FFLAGS) -c $*.e
        -rm -f $*.e

.f~.f:
        $(GET) $(GFLAGS) -p $< > $*.f

.f~.o:
        $(GET) $(GFLAGS) -p $< > $*.f
        $(FC) $(FFLAGS) -c $*.f
        -rm -f $*.f

.r.o:
        $(FC) $(FFLAGS) -c $<

.e.o:
        $(FC) $(FFLAGS) -c $<

.f.o:
        $(FC) $(FFLAGS) -c $<

.c~.c:
        $(GET) $(GFLAGS) -p $< > $*.c

.c~.o:
        $(GET) $(GFLAGS) -p $< > $*.c
        $(CC) $(CFLAGS) -c $*.c
        -rm -f $*.c

.c.o:
        $(CC) $(CFLAGS) -c $<

.sh~:
        $(GET) $(GFLAGS) -p $< > $*.sh
        cp $*.sh $*
        -rm -f $*.sh
.sh:
        cp $< $@
.r~:
        $(GET) $(GFLAGS) -p $< > $*.r
        $(FC) -n $(FFLAGS) $*.r -o $*
        -rm -f $*.r
.r:
        $(FC) $(FFLAGS) $(LDFLAGS) $< -o $@
```

```
.e~:
     $(GET) $(GFLAGS) -p $< > $*.e
     $(FC) -n $(FFLAGS) $*.e -o $*
     -rm -f $*.e

.e:
     $(FC) $(FFLAGS) $(LDFLAGS) $< -o $@

.f~:
     $(GET) $(GFLAGS) -p $< > $*.f
     $(FC) -n $(FFLAGS) $*.f -o $*
     -rm -f $*.f

.f:
     $(FC) $(FFLAGS) $(LDFLAGS) $< -o $@

.c~:
     $(GET) $(GFLAGS) -p $< > $*.c
     $(CC) -n $(CFLAGS) $*.c -o $*
     -rm -f $*.c

.c:
     $(CC) $(CFLAGS) $(LDFLAGS) $< -o $@

.SUFFIXES: .o .c .c~ .f .f~ .e .e~ .r .r~ .y .y~ .l .l~ \
.s .s~ .sh .sh~ .h .h~
```

C

A Large Makefile

The following description file controls the generation of "server" and "client" programs that are part of a complete Ethernet software product. A client in this context means a program that is accessible to users and performs some function across the network—for example, the *rlogin* program that carries out remote logins. A server is the program on the "other end" of the client request—for example, the *rlogind* program that accepts and responds to remote login requests.

The files in this software project are maintained under SCCS control. SCCS files are maintained in a sub-directory called "SCCS", and are pulled out of that directory whenever they need to be modified, compiled, or otherwise handled. See Chapter 3 for a limited discussion of SCCS. More detailed information about SCCS is available in the *UNIX Programmer's Manual*.

At the end of the sample makefile is a figure that shows the directory structure reflected in the description file. In this figure, the "Current Directory" contains the description file (shown on the far right) that is reproduced here. A second description file—which can be invoked from the first—is contained in the "FTP" sub-directory. Note that the entire hierarchy of files treated in the main description file shown here is only one of a number of sub-trees in the overall networking software project.

```
RELEASE=2.0                        # Product release number
SCCSREL=3                          # SCCS version number
SOURCE=/usr/src/COMM

SRCDIR=${SOURCE}/netser

SERVERDEST=/etc/net
CLIENTDEST=/usr/bin

# The "kit" is the release version of the software, stored on
# disk in a form ready for distribution to customers
KITDESTDIR=/kit/cm-50/${RELEASE}
SERVERKIT=${KITDESTDIR}/${SERVERDEST}
CLIENTKIT=${KITDESTDIR}/${CLIENTDEST}

# Directories with header, or "include" files
INCOMM=../h
INCRT=/usr/include

CFLAGS= -O -I${INCOMM} -I${INCRT} ${INCLUDE} ${DEFINE}
LDFLAGS=
LIBES=

SERVERS=   netd rloginserver rshserver timeserver uucpserver \
           telnetserver ftpserver tftpserver rwhod

# Some clients are owned by "root", others by "bin"
ROOTCLIENTS=   rcp rlogin rsh
BINCLIENTS=    rtime telnet ftp tftp rwho ruptime whereami

CLIENTS= ${ROOTCLIENTS} ${BINCLIENTS}
PROGS=   ${SERVERS} ${CLIENTS}

FILES=   netd.c rloginserv.c rshserver.c timeserver.c \
     uucpserver.c telnetserv.c tftpserver.c rwhod.c \
     rwhod.h rcp.c rlogin.c rsh.c rtime.c telnet.c \
     tftp.c rwho.c ruptime.c whereami.c

# get files from SCCS control
```

```
GET= sccs -d ${SRCDIR} get -r${SCCSREL} -t


.DEFAULT:
     $(GET) $@

all:              ${PROGS}
servers:          ${SERVERS}
clients:          ${CLIENTS}
source:           ${FILES}

# Server programs--SCCS source dependencies
netd.o:           netd.c
rloginserv.o:     rloginserv.c
rshserver.o:      rshserver.c
timeserver.o:     timeserver.c
uucpserver.o:     uucpserver.c
telnetserv.o:     telnetserv.c
tftpserver.o:     tftpserver.c
rexecserv.o:      rexecserv.c
rwhod.o:          rwhod.c rwhod.h

netd:             netd.o
        ${CC} ${LDFLAGS} -o $@ netd.o ${LIBES} -ljobs

rloginserver:     rloginserv.o
        ${CC} ${LDFLAGS} -o $@ rloginserv.o ${LIBES}

rshserver:        rshserver.o
          ${CC} ${LDFLAGS} -o $@ rshserver.o ${LIBES}

timeserver:       timeserver.o
        ${CC} ${LDFLAGS} -o $@ timeserver.o ${LIBES}

uucpserver:       uucpserver.o
        ${CC} ${LDFLAGS} -o $@ uucpserver.o ${LIBES}

telnetserver:     telnetserv.o
        ${CC} ${LDFLAGS} -o $@ telnetserv.o ${LIBES}

tftpserver:       tftpserver.o
        ${CC} ${LDFLAGS} -o $@ tftpserver.o ${LIBES}

rexecserver:      rexecserv.o
        ${CC} ${LDFLAGS} -o $@ rexecserv.o ${LIBES}

# In following line /tmp is used to force execution of commands
# /tmp is always more recently modified than ftpserver
ftpserver:        /tmp
        INCOMM=`cd ${INCOMM}; pwd` INCRT=`cd ${INCRT}; \
        pwd` cd FTP; make ../ftpserver SCCSREL=${SCCSREL} \
```

```
            LIBES="${LIBES}" \
                INCOMM=$$INCOMM INCRT=$$INCRT \
                SOURCE="${SOURCE}" INCLUDE="${INCLUDE}" \
                DEFINE="${DEFINE}"

rwhod:  rwhod.o
        ${CC} ${LDFLAGS} -o $@ rwhod.o ${LIBES} -ljobs

# Client programs--SCCS source dependencies
rcp.o:          rcp.c
rlogin.o:       rlogin.c
rsh.o:          rsh.c
rtime.o:        rtime.c
telnet.o:       telnet.c
tftp.o:         tftp.c
rwho.o:         rwho.c rwhod.h
ruptime.o:      ruptime.c rwhod.h
whereami.o:     whereami.c

rcp:            rcp.o
        ${CC} ${LDFLAGS} -o $@ rcp.o ${LIBES} -lndir

rlogin:         rlogin.o
        ${CC} ${LDFLAGS} -o $@ rlogin.o ${LIBES} -ljobs

rsh:            rsh.o
        ${CC} ${LDFLAGS} -o $@ rsh.o ${LIBES} -ljobs

rtime:          rtime.o
        ${CC} ${LDFLAGS} -o $@ rtime.o ${LIBES}

telnet:         telnet.o
        ${CC} ${LDFLAGS} -o $@ telnet.o ${LIBES}

tftp:           tftp.o
        ${CC} ${LDFLAGS} -o $@ tftp.o ${LIBES}

ftp:    /tmp
        INCOMM=`cd ${INCOMM}; pwd` INCRT=`cd ${INCRT}; \
        pwd` cd FTP; make ../ftp SCCSREL=${SCCSREL} \
        LIBES="${LIBES}" \
                INCOMM=$$INCOMM INCRT=$$INCRT \
                SOURCE="${SOURCE}" INCLUDE="${INCLUDE}" \
                DEFINE="${DEFINE}"

rwho:           rwho.o
        ${CC} ${LDFLAGS} -o $@ rwho.o ${LIBES} -lndir

ruptime:        ruptime.o
        ${CC} ${LDFLAGS} -o $@ ruptime.o ${LIBES} -lndir
```

```
whereami:        whereami.o
        ${CC} ${LDFLAGS} -o $@ whereami.o ${LIBES}

#
# Miscellany
#
clean:
        rm -f ${PROGS} *.o
        cd FTP; make clean

# Build the actual distribution kit
kit:    all
        cp ${SERVERS} ${SERVERKIT}
        cd ${SERVERKIT}; strip ${SERVERS}
        cd ${SERVERKIT}; chown bin ${SERVERS}
        cd ${SERVERKIT}; chgrp bin ${SERVERS}
        cd ${SERVERKIT}; chmod 744 ${SERVERS}
        cp ${CLIENTS} ${CLIENTKIT}
        cd ${CLIENTKIT}; strip ${CLIENTS}
        cd ${CLIENTKIT}; chown root ${ROOTCLIENTS}
        cd ${CLIENTKIT}; chown bin ${BINCLIENTS}
        cd ${CLIENTKIT}; chgrp bin ${CLIENTS}
        cd ${CLIENTKIT}; chmod 4755 ${ROOTCLIENTS}
        cd ${CLIENTKIT}; chmod 755 ${BINCLIENTS}
        mv ${CLIENTKIT}/rsh ${KITDESTDIR}/update
        mv ${CLIENTKIT}/rtime ${KITDESTDIR}/bin
```

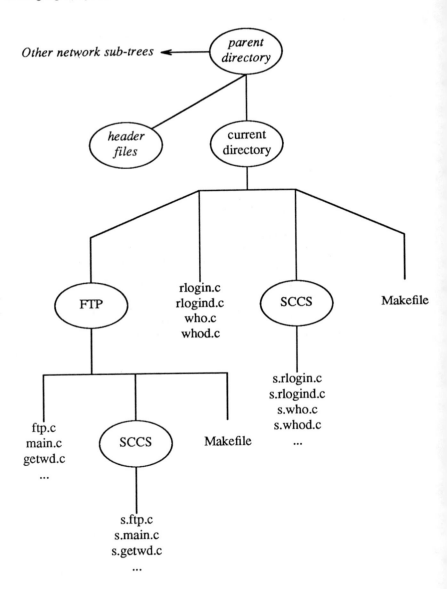

Hierarchy of Files Described in Sample Makefile

Index

.c suffix 23
.DEFAULT (pseudo-target) 41
.f suffix 23
.IGNORE (pseudo-target) 39
$ (MAKE) macro 52
.mk suffix 36
.o suffix 23
.PRECIOUS (pseudo-target) 38
.s suffix 23
.SUFFIXES line 24

A

arguments
  in command lines 35
  macro definitions 36
  option flags 36

assembly language
  source files 23
asterisk (*) 13
at sign (@) 37

B

-b flag 40, 55
backslash (\) 11
blank lines
  in description files 7
Bourne shell 10
braces ({ })
  in macro definitions 16
brackets ([ ]) 13

Colophon

Our look is the result of reader comments, our own experimentation, and distribution channels.

Distinctive covers complement our distinctive approach to UNIX documentation, breathing personality and life into potentially dry subjects. UNIX and its attendant programs can be unruly beasts. Nutshell Handbooks help you tame them.

The animal featured on the cover of *Managing Projects with Make* is a potto.

Edie Freedman designed this cover and the entire UNIX bestiary that appears on other Nutshell Handbooks. The beasts themselves are adapted from 19th-century engravings from the Dover Pictorial Archive.

Linda Lamb designed the page layout for the Nutshell Handbooks. The text of this book is set in Times Roman; headings are Helvetica®; examples are Courier. Text was prepared using SoftQuad's *sqtroff* formatter. Figures are produced with a Macintosh™. Printing is done on an Apple LaserWriter®.